THE HEALTH AND HAPPINESS HANDBOOK COMPANION JOURNAL

DANIELLE AITKEN

Copyright © 2022 by Project Heart Publishing.

All rights reserved.

No part of this book may be reproduced in any form or by any electronic or mechanical means, including information storage and retrieval systems, without written permission from the author, except for the use of brief quotations in a book review.

The author and publisher have made every effort to contact copyright holders for material used in this book. Any person or organisation that may have been overlooked should contact the publisher.

NATIONAL LIBRARY OF AUSTRALIA
A catalogue record of this book is available from: www.trove.nla.gov.au

The Health and Happiness Handbook Companion Journal Author: Danielle Aitken

Editor: Julia Kaylock

Cover: Ashley Herr & Danielle Aitken

Interior design: Vellum

ISBN: 978-0-6488078-7-2(e)

ISBN: 978-0-6488078-6-5

CONTENTS

The Health & Happiness Handbook	v
CHANGE	vii
Introduction	ix
Remember	xi
DAY 1	1
Notes	5
DAY 2	6
Notes	8
DAY 3	9
Notes	11
DAY 4	12
Notes	14
DAY 5	15
Notes	17
DAY 6	18
Notes	21
DAY 7	22
Notes	24
DAY 8	25
Notes	27
DAY 9	28
Notes	30
DAY 10	31
Notes	33
DAY 11	34
Notes	36
DAY 12	37
Notes	39
DAY 13	40
Notes	42
DAY 14	43
Notes	45
DAY 15	46

Notes	48
DAY 16	49
Notes	51
DAY 17	52
Notes	54
DAY 18	55
Notes	57
DAY 19	58
Notes	60
DAY 20	61
Notes	63
DAY 21	64
Notes	66
Final Review	67
About the Author	69

THE HEALTH & HAPPINESS HANDBOOK
COMPANION JOURNAL

Change happens because of what you DO in 'this' moment

Danielle Aitken.
Counsellor, Clinical Hypnotherapist, R.N.,R.M
National President Australian Hypnotherapists' Association

CHANGE

If you want to CREATE something different you need to DO something different.

Danielle Aitken

INTRODUCTION

Welcome to your 21 Day Health and Happiness Handbook Companion Journal.

It is often estimated that it takes anywhere from 21 – 84 days to create new habits, some estimates are longer than that. Naturally the more pleasurable a habit, the more likely we are to keep doing it. Therefore, when seeking change, there is no one size fits all. Habits are created through repetition and focus of attention. What this means is we must give our new desired changes the same focus of attention and repetition that created our problems in the first place.

Thus, It is imperative to remember that if perseverance and repetition created your old habits, that same determination will be required to create your *new* habits.

This **Companion Journal** is designed to be used in conjunction with the principles, helpful techniques and daily practices presented in the accompanying **Health and Happiness Handbook.**

Many of the techniques described in the handbook are designed to interrupt your old patterns of thinking and feeling, effectively leading to neural rewiring of your brain for the changes you desire.

INTRODUCTION

Before we begin, please answer in the space provided:

On a scale of 1-10 where 1= least effect and 10 = maximum effect

How would you rate:

- your current happiness levels:
- your current contentment levels:
- your current level of gratitude:
- your current ability to be mindful:
- your current ability to relax:
- your current anxiety levels:
- your current depression levels:
- your current dissatisfaction levels:

REMEMBER

The moment you become 'aware' of anything, be it a thought, feeling or behaviour,
you are immediately in a position of choice.
What you choose in that moment will determine your outcomes.

∼

LET'S BEGIN

DAY 1
WEEK ONE

As you begin your 21-day Health and Happiness Companion Journal, you may like to review what we have learned in the **Health and Happiness Handbook**, Part One: *The Power Of Thought*.

It is important to remember, your thoughts *are* powerful, and *will* impact upon your outcomes in either positive or negative ways, depending on your choices. Therefore, when you are seeking to create change it is imperative to remember that if you begin your day by thinking the same limiting thoughts about yesterday's problems, or by focusing on the same limiting feelings and beliefs, you will be chemically, emotionally and physically recreating yesterday with all its perceived problems and concerns today, in the present moment, when probably much of it is not actually happening.

Why?

Your powerful subconscious mind cannot tell the difference between what you are imagining to be true, and what *is* true. It will therefore immediately respond to whatever it is you focus your attention on, be it real or imagined, as though it *is* true. What's more, neurologically you will also be strengthening the neural pathways that have been keeping those same troublesome thoughts, feelings and behaviours firing and wiring.

As stated in **The Health and Happiness Handbook**, awareness, knowledge, and understanding are the key components to creating change. We can use the principle of 'linking', as described in the handbook, to begin to establish new habits to your morning routine as soon as you open your eyes.

DAILY BREATH PRACTICE

Today and every day for the next 21 days and beyond, choose to begin your day by taking four long slow breaths when you open your eyes in the morning and at three other times during your day.

First, choose a breath technique from Part Two of The **Health and Happiness Handbook** Part Two: in the *Breath Techniques and Practices* section, that feels comfortable and works well for you.

To complete this important exercise, each day as soon as you wake up, you will take four long slow relaxing breaths. You can repeat this at other times during your day; choose a specific time or a particular activity that you can connect the breath practice to. This identified time and / or activity will act as a reminder, prompting you to remember to practise your breath technique. Effectively this will also create a situational anchor or link, as discussed in the *Practices to Enhance Neuroplasticity* section of the handbook.

For example, you may link the breath practice to:

- waiting for the kettle to boil,
- before or after you eat; breakfast / lunch / dinner,
- before or after a specific task,
- when you go to the bathroom, or
- when you have finished brushing your teeth.

Each time you run your pre-existing habit, it will act as a reminder to take a breath, which effectively takes you out of stress mode and connects you to a state of calmness and clarity.

Once you have taken four long, slow, calming breaths first thing in the morning, turn your attention to the next activity.

DAILY GRATITUDE REFLECTION

Research has demonstrated that a daily gratitude practice produces beneficial effects which lead to improvements in our physical and emotional health.

For this reason, I will ask you to establish a daily gratitude routine. Please refer to **The Health and Happiness Handbook** Part One: *Gratitude*, and Part Two: *Daily Gratitude Practices*.

Each day for the next 21 days, begin your day by focusing your attention on **five** things you are grateful for, which may include:

- the big things
- the small things
- the things we generally take for granted.

When you awaken in the morning, immediately after you have practised your breath technique described above, take a moment to reflect on these five things.

This will become a daily morning practice.

WHAT WENT WELL TODAY?

In the evening, choose to reflect on what went well for you during your day. You may like to discuss these things with other family members. This positive discussion changes the often-negative predisposition we have of leaning toward, or focusing on, those things that we perceive to have gone wrong in our day.

Activity

- Reflect on one thing that went well in your day.
- Take time to discuss this with someone you care for.
- How did discussing these things with someone else effect you?

Place some thoughts in the section provided.

- *For electronic journals: please use your preferred method to make notes.*

NOTES

DAY 2

For the next 21 days and beyond you will be required to complete the three new practices that you implemented on day one, PLUS daily additional tasks.

By the end of week one these practices will be beginning to become more familiar and easier for you to complete effortlessly.

Please note that although it may look like a lot, most of these practices can be completed in a few minutes a day.

<u>Your daily practices</u> for every day, as described on day one are:

- Daily breath practice: 4 breaths
- Daily gratitude reflection: 5 things
- Evening reflection: What went well today?

Activity for Day 2

Interrupting old limiting habits and patterns.

Awareness is the key to creating change, and according to the principles of quantum physics, **'like attracts like'**, thus when we repetitively focus on our problems and limitations, we are inadvertently inviting more of the same. Combine this with a little neuroplasticity, remember the cow track analogy in the handbook, where we note that the more activity a neural pathway responsible for running your problem gets, the stronger and more permanent it becomes. You may be beginning to understand that it is imperative to interrupt these old unhelpful habits and patterns as soon as you notice them.

Today we begin the practice of being aware, and actively interrupting our patterns and habits that are redundant or unhelpful.

- Step 1: Awareness
- Step 2: Challenge
- Step 3: Interrupt the pattern and redirect your attention.

Please refer to **The Health and Happiness Handbook** Part Two: *Pattern Interrupt* for full instructions on how to practise this technique.

Use the space provided to reflect on your observations.

- *For electronic journals: please use your preferred method to make notes.*

NOTES

DAY 3

YOUR DAILY PRACTICES

- **Daily breath practice: 4 breaths**
- **Daily gratitude reflection: 5 things**
- **Evening reflection: What went well today?**

PLUS

- **Practise the 'pattern Interrupt' technique as required throughout your day.**

Today and every day, pay particular attention to your self-talk.

To create change we need to identify the processes and habits that have been keeping us stuck in old self-defeating patterns and beliefs.

It is important to remember that the powerful sub-conscious mind which responds to every thought we have in physical, chemical, and emotional ways, is constantly eavesdropping on all of our internal dialogue.

Words to be aware of are those listed in **The Health and Happiness Handbook** Part One: *You Are What You Think: Self-fulfilling Prophesies* Listed under: *Common Negative Automatic Thoughts* and *Statements, Words, and Phrases to be aware of.*

Activity for Day 3

Today, bring awareness to your internal dialogue. Notice any self-sabotaging, repetitive or negative self-talk as you remember that what you say to yourself are instructions to your sub-conscious mind.

Things to consider:

- Notice your repetitive, negative, or automatic thoughts
- How often were you able to challenge these limiting thoughts / feelings / beliefs?
- How often have you been telling yourself and / or believing these things?
- Would you accept it if someone else said these things to you?
- How do you feel about what you have observed?

In the space provided: Write down any negative statements, thoughts and / or beliefs that you became aware of today.

- *For electronic journals: please use your preferred method to make notes.*

NOTES

DAY 4

YOUR DAILY PRACTICES

- **Daily breath practice: 4 breaths**
- **Daily gratitude reflection: 5 things**
- **Evening reflection: What went well today?**

PLUS

- **Remember to check your self-talk throughout the day and practise the pattern interrupt as required.**

Activity for Day 4

Building on the activity of yesterday, when you open your eyes in the morning, be aware of your immediate thoughts. Remember if you think yesterday's thoughts about yesterday's problems you are dragging yesterday into today when most of those 'worrying concerns' are probably not happening.

If concerning thoughts do come to mind, ask yourself, is there anything to be gained by ruminating over these old repetitive thoughts. If the answer is no, put them to one side, take a purposeful breath, relaxing into the exhalation, and as you step out of stress mode, redirect your attention to your new routine.

WHO DO I CHOOSE TO BE TODAY?

From today, when you wake up in the morning, ask yourself the question: "**Who do I choose to be today?**"

- Who do I want to be today?
- What will that look like?
- What will it feel like?
- What will be different?
- What do I want to achieve today?

∼

Place some thoughts in the section provided.

You will refer to these notes in tomorrow's activity, *Creating Your Solution State*.

- *For electronic journals: please use your preferred method to make notes.*

NOTES

DAY 5

YOUR DAILY PRACTICES

- **Daily breath practice: 4 breaths**
- **Daily gratitude reflection: 5 things**
- **Morning reflection: Who do I choose to be today?**

PLUS

- **Check your self-talk / use pattern interrupt throughout the day**
- **Evening reflection: What went well today?**

It is important once again to notice, that although this may seem to be a lot of activities, when practised routinely, it becomes a habit that will only take a few minutes of your day, however these changes will make a massive difference to your outcomes when practised regularly.

Today choose a different breath technique to practise from The **Health and Happiness Handbook:** *Breath Techniques and Practices*

Activity for Day 5

Today have a conversation with someone and practise <u>Mindful Listening</u> as described in **The Health and Happiness Handbook** Part Two: *Mindful Practices*.

Also, during your day:

- Remember in times of stress to take a breath paying particular attention to the exhalation and relaxing into it.
- Notice when your breath practice has been helpful to change the way you were feeling.
- Notice how focusing on gratitude and appreciation has altered the way you feel throughout your day.
- Notice how mindful listening positively enhances your conversation.

<u>**Use the space provided to make notes**</u>: Reflect on what you have noticed from your practices thus far.

- *For electronic Journals: please use your preferred method to make notes.*

NOTES

DAY 6

YOUR DAILY PRACTICES

- **Daily breath practice: 4 breaths**
- **Daily gratitude reflection: 5 things**
- **Morning reflection: Who do I choose to be today?**

PLUS

- **Check your self-talk / use pattern interrupt throughout the day**
- **Evening reflection: What went well today?**

Activity for Day 6

CREATE YOUR OWN SOLUTION STATE

Please refer to **The Health and Happiness Handbook** Part Two: *Creating Your Solution State* section, to find the full instructions on how to create your own solution state.

After reviewing this information and your notes from yesterday's activity, use the space provided below to create your own solution state.

On the left-hand side of the page: dot point all the things you consider to be a part of the current problem or situation you wish to address.

On the right-hand side of the page: dot point how you **will** feel, think, and behave when the old issue no longer exists, we call this your solution state.

Remembering what we have said about the subconscious mind and the power of your thoughts. **It is important to use ONLY solution-focused language in your solution state.**

Please refer to **The Health and Happiness Handbook** Part One: *The Power of Thought*, and Part Two: *Your Thoughts are Powerful*.

When you have a good sense of what this new 'you' will look, feel and be like, 'step' right into your solution state and pretend or imagine for that moment that you are already living it.

It is important to not just think about your solution state, but to really 'feel' and fully embrace it, as though you have already achieved it. Remember that your powerful sub-conscious mind cannot tell the difference between what is real, and what you are imagining to be real, thus it responds to every thought you have as though it is true.

Focus on this version of you every day by imagining or pretending that you have already achieved it. Make it vivid, make it as real as you can imagine. Get creative here. Your solution state may change the more you focus on it. Get familiar with who it is you are creating.

You don't have to 'see' it if you are not visual. Just imagine it in any way that works for you, as you continue to get a real sense of this future you.

When you do this correctly, you are becoming a visionary, creating your future as you want it to be.

Place thoughts / feelings and comments in the section provided.

- *For electronic journals: please use your preferred method to make notes.*

What is my **PROBLEM** / What is my **SOLUTION**

NOTES

DAY 7

YOUR DAILY PRACTICES

- **Daily breath practice: 4 breaths**
- **Daily gratitude reflection: 5 things**
- **Morning reflection: Who do I choose to be today?**

PLUS

- **Remember to check your self-talk throughout the day.**
- **Evening reflection: What went well today?**

Activity for Day 7

Today after you have done your four morning breaths and created a calm state, bring to mind the 'you' of your solution state. Take between one or two minutes to step into this and truly immerse yourself in the details of it. For those moments, really imagine that you have already achieved it. Connect to the empowered emotions of this version of you.

After you have connected to your solution state, as described above, ask yourself: What is one thing you can do today, that will make a difference in how you experience your tomorrow?

At the end of the day ask yourself the question, what specifically did I do today that moved me closer toward my solution state?

Use the space provided to write notes and observations.

- *For electronic journals: please use your preferred method to make notes.*

NOTES

DAY 8
WEEK TWO

YOUR DAILY PRACTICES

- **Daily breath practice: From this week increase this activity to 8 breaths**
- **Daily gratitude reflection: 5 things**
- **Morning reflection: Who do I choose to be today?**

PLUS

- **Take two minutes to step into your solution state as though you have already achieved it, remember to really connect to the empowered feelings of this state.**
- **Check your self-talk throughout the day**
- **Evening reflection: What went well today?**

Activity for Day 8

Practise a mindful technique from **The Health and Happiness Handbook** *Mindful Practices* section.

Write in the space provided any daily reflections

- *For electronic journals: please use your preferred method to make notes.*

- What unhelpful thoughts was I able to challenge and interrupt today?
- What three things went well for me today?
- What did I do differently today that will lead me to my solution state?
- What slipped past my awareness?
- How did this make me feel?

Please Note: Today, if you noticed at any point that you were automatically running an old habit, be it negative self-talk or a limiting belief or behaviour, the moment you became aware of it was your opportunity to choose something else without judgment. Each time you do this you weaken the old neural pathway that has previously kept your old habit firing and wiring.

NOTES

DAY 9

YOUR DAILY PRACTICES

- **Daily breath practice: 8 breaths**
- **Daily gratitude reflection: 5 things**
- **Morning reflection: Who do I choose to be today?**

PLUS

- **Check your self-talk throughout the day**
- **Evening reflection: What went well today?**
- **Take two minutes to step into your solution state as though You have already achieved it, remember to really connect to the empowered feelings of this state.**

Activity for Day 9

Throughout your day remember to take note of any negative, automatic or limiting thoughts.

You may like to list some of these thoughts in the space provided to bring more conscious awareness to them.

Remember awareness is the key to creating change, as soon as you are aware of anything, you are in a position of choice. What you do from there will determine your outcomes.

Notice whether these thoughts are becoming less frequent, as you continue to interrupt the patterns that have kept them running.

Make notes in the space provided.

- *For electronic journals: please use your preferred method to make notes.*

NOTES

DAY 10

YOUR DAILY PRACTICES

- **Daily breath practice: 8 breaths**
- **Daily gratitude reflection: 5 things**
- **Morning reflection: Who do I choose to be today?**

PLUS

- **Check your self-talk throughout the day**
- **Evening reflection: What went well today?**
- **Take two minutes to step into your solution state as though You have already achieved it, remember to really connect to the empowered feelings of this state.**

It has now been 10 days and you are now becoming more aware of your old habit of focusing your attention on old repetitive, outdated or negative, automatic thoughts.

Remember to do your breath work throughout your day.

A minimum of four to eight breaths at least four times a day is a wonderful place to start.

You may choose to do this more often.

How many times would you estimate that you became aware today that you were focusing on old negative habitual thoughts or running old habits?

How many times were you able to effectively challenge them?

What are you noticing about these thoughts and habits?

Specifically:

- Are they the same repetitive thoughts as yesterday?
- How often are they coming?
- Are they becoming less frequent?
- Is it easier to change your focus than it was one week ago?

What needs more awareness?

The key is to get curious about these things **without** judgement and to simply change your focus.

Activity for Day 10

Write your observations in the space provided.

- *For electronic journals: please use your preferred method to make notes.*

NOTES

DAY 11

YOUR DAILY PRACTICES

- **Daily breath practice: 8 breaths**
- **Daily gratitude reflection: 5 things**
- **Morning reflection: Who do I choose to be today?**

PLUS

- **Check your self-talk throughout the day**
- **Evening reflection: What went well today?**
- **Take two minutes to step into your solution state as though You have already achieved it, remember to really connect to the empowered feelings of this state.**

Let's start the day with a mindful wake up. REMEMBER your thoughts create your state of mind. Your state of mind will impact directly on your outcomes. So, take a moment to really focus on the following….

- Who do you want to be today?
- What will that look like?
- What will that feel like?
- What will you be doing that will make a difference?
- What will you no longer be doing that will make a difference?
- What thoughts will be helpful?
- What thoughts will no longer be helpful?
- What have you noticed you have been able to implement in the last week that has made a difference to your daily experience?
- How do you feel you are going?

Activity for Day 11

Experiment with a meditation practice of your choosing from **The Health and Happiness Handbook.**

- Did this practice meet your expectations?
- What was enjoyable?
- What was challenging?

Write your thoughts in the space provided.

- *For electronic journals: please use your preferred method to make notes.*

NOTES

DAY 12

YOUR DAILY PRACTICES

- **Daily breath practice: 8 breaths**
- **Daily gratitude reflection: 5 things**
- **Take two minutes to step into your solution state as though You have already achieved it.**

PLUS

- **Evening reflection: What went well today?**
- **Remember to check your self-talk throughout the day**

Activity for Day 12

- Today reflect on your most important values.
- List your top 3 values.
- Now reflect on the question: How do my daily thoughts / feelings and behaviours honour my values?

Make notes in the section provided

- *For electronic Journals: please use your preferred method to make notes.*

NOTES

DAY 13

YOUR DAILY PRACTICES

- **Daily breath practice: 8 breaths**
- **Daily gratitude reflection: 5 things**
- **Take two minutes to step into your solution state as though You have already achieved it**

PLUS

- **Evening reflection: What went well today?**
- **Remember to check your self-talk throughout the day**

Activity for day 13

Please refer to **The Health and Happiness Handbook** Part 2 *Mindful Practices*: *Utilise all your senses to be fully present in nature.*

Today, take yourself outside into the great outdoors. You may be lucky enough to have a beautiful garden on your doorstep, however this is not necessary, you can do this activity under a tree in the middle of a busy city or anywhere you can connect to nature in some way.

Refer to the steps in the handbook and get curious about what you can notice in the present moment.

Reflect on this experience and make notes in the section provided.

- *For electronic journals: please use your preferred method to make notes.*

NOTES

DAY 14

Well done, you have now reached two weeks and your daily practices will now be becoming your new daily habits.

Remember to continue being mindful of your thoughts, self-editing negative thoughts, feelings and behaviours without judgment as required and redirecting your attention to more helpful thoughts, feelings and behaviours.

One of the most important things you can do this week and beyond, is to continue each day to remember who you are choosing to become. Make this image of you vivid, colourful, and real. Move right into it each and every day imagining or pretending for that moment that you have already achieved it. Really feel the feelings of this 'you' and fully embrace it utilising your powerful subconscious mind.

Activity for Day 14

From today, take a little longer to fully embrace your solution state reflection every day. Each time you do this you are moving closer towards the person you are choosing to become, whilst simultaneously strengthening the neural pathway that is firing and wiring every time you do this practice.

To reinforce your learning, you may wish to review the section on creating your solution state in **The Health and Happiness Handbook** Part 1: *Your Solution State* and Part 2: *Creating your Solution State*

Activity: Go to my YouTube channel **Danielle Aitken Clinical Hypnotherapist** and click on the *Relaxation Body Scan*.

Complete the body scan, and then take some time to fully immerse yourself into your solution state. This is a form of self-hypnosis, but remember it is essential that you not only think about the person you are choosing to be, but also that you really 'embrace the feelings' of this 'you', as though you have already achieved it.

In the section provided, write your reflections.

- *For electronic journals: please use your preferred method to make notes.*

NOTES

DAY 15
WEEK THREE

Continue with your daily practices.

If you enjoyed the relaxation body scan, feel free to continue doing this every day. You may also get curious as to the many meditation apps available and many YouTube meditations to explore. Remember there is no one size fits all here, find the one that works for you.

∽

Activity for Day 15

Today, really focus your attention on being mindful.

Mindfulness is a practice that can increase our enjoyment of life in all areas of our day.

We have spoken and practised being mindful of our thoughts over the last two weeks. We have also practised breath techniques and body scans. Today let's see if you can have a mindful day.

. . .

Remember you can be mindful when:

- eating
- drinking
- speaking
- walking
- sitting
- washing dishes
- sweeping floors
- being in nature

You can practise mindfulness anywhere and at any time.

To immerse yourself in mindfulness over a whole mindful day you may find it beneficial to turn off all social media for 24 hours.

See how you go!

Write your reflections in the space provided.

- *For electronic journals: please use your preferred method to make notes.*

NOTES

DAY 16

Continue with your daily practices.

How did you go with your mindful day?

Was it easy or harder than you thought?

It's not unusual for it to be more difficult than you expected, but we don't want to judge these attempts. To do so takes the focus of your attention away from your solution state. Any time you noticed that you had slipped back into old habits, is a time that you became aware! When you become aware of anything it means you have put yourself in a position of choice, from this position you get the opportunity to decide what you do next. I wonder, what did *you* choose?

Activity for Day 16

Today let's continue our mindful practices, perhaps take a *mindful walk in nature* or even stand in the garden for five minutes and practise *Mindful Viewing* or *Utilising all your senses to be fully in nature.*

All of these practices can be found in **The Health and Happiness Handbook** Part: 2 *Mindful Practices*

- What have you noticed is changing for you?
- What are you doing differently?
- What are you doing less often?
- What are you doing more often?
- How are you managing to overcome those old repetitive thoughts, feelings, beliefs?

Use the space provided to write your reflections

- *For electronic journals: please use your preferred method to make notes.*

NOTES

DAY 17

Don't forget to continue you daily practices. You may like to explore the many different breath techniques mentioned in **The Health and Happiness Handbook** or any others that you may have discovered.

Today we are going to focus on gratitude. I hope you have enjoyed your daily gratitude practice each morning, and I wonder if you have discovered that it has become easier to identify the things you have to be grateful for?

Today we are going to build on your existing gratitude practice.

∽

Activity for Day 17

Today choose a gratitude object to carry with you. Please refer to **The Health and Happiness Handbook** Part 2: *Daily Gratitude Practices*.

Each time you see the gratitude object throughout your day, take a moment to give thanks for something in your life that you are grateful for.

- If you sit at a desk, have your object in plain sight.
- If you are out and about, have it in a place that it will be noticed often. For example: with your car keys / in your purse / in your pocket / in the car in plain sight / in the nappy bag.

At the end of the day reflect on how this activity made you feel.

Is this something you will choose to continue?

Did it change the way you interacted with others during the day?

Write your reflections in the space provided.

- *For electronic journals: please use your preferred method to make notes.*

NOTES

DAY 18

Continue your daily practices

Day 18 and we are now two and a half weeks into your 21-day Health and Happiness Companion Journal. How are you feeling?

Today, we are continuing our gratitude practice, so you may wish to continue to carry around your gratitude object with you for the next few days up to day 21 and beyond if you feel you would like to.

Activity for Day 18

If you feel moved to do so, use the space provided in the journal to write down three people for whom you are eternally grateful to for being in your life.

- *For electronic journals: please use your preferred method to make notes and complete this activity.*

Next choose one of these people and write a gratitude letter to them in the space provided, or in another space if you need more room.

Prior to commencing this task take a few moments to sit in silence and allow your breath to slow. Allow your attention to go to the area of your heart, and as you do, focus your attention on the person you have chosen. Allow yourself to really connect to the feeling of gratitude for this person. When you are really feeling the gratitude, begin writing.

Please note: this activity is for you only. You do not have to show the person who you have written about, however if you wish to, you may.

NOTES

DAY 19

Continue all your daily practices.

- How did you find the gratitude letter experience?
- Was it harder or easier than expected?
- How did it feel to fully embrace heart felt gratitude?
- Having written it, have your thoughts changed about showing the person the letter or not?

Activity for Day 19

Research shows that the act of giving is often more beneficial in the way it makes you feel than the act of receiving.

Option One:

Call or meet up with the person you wrote the gratitude letter about. Tell them there is something you want them to hear. Ask them if they could please not interrupt you while you speak.

Read them the letter.

Option Two:

If it is not possible to contact the person you wrote your gratitude letter to, *or* if you would prefer not to read them your letter, decide to do an act of kindness for your person.

If this is not possible do an act of kindness for someone else today.

Possible acts of kindness:

- pay for someone's coffee without them knowing
- buy someone a bunch of flowers
- mow a neighbour's nature strip
- smile at a stranger
- help someone with the door / their bag
- pull someone's bin in
- let someone in front of you in the shopping queue
- make your partner dinner / run them a bath
- compliment someone
- tell someone how much you appreciate them.

Be careful, choose wisely, have fun.

In the space provided: reflect on how you felt about this activity.

- *For electronic journals: please use your preferred method to make notes.*

NOTES

DAY 20

Nearly there!

How are you feeling?

You may like to reflect on what has changed for you in the last 20 days?

Don't forget your daily practices

Today we are going to focus on the benefits of connecting to your heart.

We have discussed this and experienced connecting to feelings of love and gratitude over the previous days, however today we are going to practise a heart coherence meditation.

This is a short meditation that brings together the extended neural network, when the neurons in the brain connect to the sensory neurites of the heart. This is discussed further in **The Health and Happiness Handbook** Part One: *Heart-Brain Coherence*.

This practice is based on over thirty years of research from the **Heart-Math Institute**. https://www.heartmath.org

I invite you to explore this simple technique which can be done in as little as three minutes, the positive chemical effects and benefits of which have been shown to last up to six hours in your blood.

Activity for day 20

You may like to go to my YouTube Channel: **Danielle Aitken Clinical Hypnotherapist**: *Heart Coherence Meditation* or a quick google search will bring up a large selection of similar Heart Coherence meditations. Find one that works for you.

Allow yourself to connect to feelings of gratitude, love, care and compassion while you complete this practice.

∾

In the space below reflect on your experience.

- *For electronic journals: please use your preferred method to make notes.*

NOTES

DAY 21

CONGRATULATIONS

You have made it to Day 21!

Well done.

- Did you think you would make it?
- Was it easier than you thought or was it more challenging?

Either is fine as we are now in the habit of being mindful and observing without judgement as life unfolds moment by moment.

Remember to do your daily practices today and every day moving forward. 😊

By now you have practised daily breath work and gratitude while mindfully paying attention to your thoughts, feelings and behaviours while also remaining focused on your solution state, and you may be noticing some significant changes in the way you are feeling and approaching life.

- What have you noticed?
- What has changed the most since you began 21 days ago?
- What have you been able to achieve?
- How does that feel?
- What have you found to be helpful?
- What has worked for you?
- How has your focus changed?
- What changes have you been able to implement?

Activity for Day 21

In the space provided take time to reflect on your experience over the last 21 days.

- *For electronic journals: please use your preferred method to make notes.*

NOTES

FINAL REVIEW

Please answer in the space provided

On a scale of 1-10 where 1= least effect and 10 = maximum effect

How do you now rate;

- your current happiness levels:
- your current contentment levels:
- your current level of gratitude:
- your current ability to be mindful:
- your current ability to relax:
- your current anxiety level:
- your current level of depression:
- your current dissatisfaction level:

Take notice of any changes in these scores since you made your first assessment on Day 1.

FINAL REVIEW

Please note:

The practices you have implemented over the last 21 days are now becoming well established as your new daily routines and habits. However this is by no means the end, in many ways it is just the beginning.

Remember, awareness is the key.

If you inadvertently slip back to old habits, do not judge yourself, simply notice it and choose something else.

> Beneficial change **only** happens when we choose to do something differently.

Now that you have discovered that you *are* in control of your thoughts, your feelings and your behaviours, through the practice of mindful awareness and purposefully choosing change, you can continue to delight in discovering that you *are* also in control of your outcomes in many positive ways.

I hope you will enjoy exploring these practices further as you mindfully step into life, each and every day, creating the changes you desire.

With Love
Danielle

ABOUT THE AUTHOR

I am passionate about human potential and the ability we have to heal, mind and body

Danielle Aitken

www.ingramcontent.com/pod-product-compliance
Lightning Source LLC
Chambersburg PA
CBHW020330010526
44107CB00054B/2048